Dear Dog, Love Always.

Stick your favourite
photo here

Dear

....

Love always,

....

INTRODUCTION

Having a dog is one of life's pure joys. The way they greet you like you're the best part of their day, every day. Their loyalty, their quirks, their tail-wagging happiness… it's all unforgettable, even if you never write it down.

But what if you did?

This journal is a space to say the things your dog can't read but already understands. A place for letters, reflections, and small moments of gratitude. Along the way, you'll also find gentle affirmations and stories of other dogs who, just like yours, left lasting pawprints in someone's life.

Whether you're writing about something silly they did this morning, or a memory you never want to forget, every word is a reminder of the bond you share.

One day, when you look back at these pages, you'll be glad you took the time to notice the love that's always been there - quiet, constant, and wagging at your side.

Love always,

Jocelyn Nguyen
fellow dog lover

I am *lucky* to
be loved by
a dog like you.

DATE / /

The first time *I met you*, I remember thinking...

DATE / /

Today, I want to *thank you* for...

DATE / /

What your name *means to me*

WHY I CHOSE IT / HOW YOU GOT IT

NICKNAMES I CALL YOU

WHAT YOUR NAME REMINDS ME OF NOW

Hachikō

The dog who waited for nine years...

In 1920s Tokyo, a golden-coated Akita named Hachiko would walk his owner to the train station each morning and return every afternoon to greet him. One day, his owner didn't come back. He had passed away unexpectedly at work.

But Hachiko didn't know that.

So he kept waiting.

And kept waiting.

For the next nine years, Hachiko returned to the station every single day - rain, snow or sunshine - sitting patiently at the same spot. Commuters began to notice the quiet dog and were moved by his devotion. Eventually, Hachiko became a national symbol of loyalty.

Even today, a bronze statue of him still sits outside Shibuya Station, where he once waited.

DATE / /

Something *only you do* that makes you one of a kind...

DATE / /

My *favourite moments* with you...

FUNNY

SWEET

ADVENTUROUS

UNEXPECTED

DATE / /

One thing about you I'll *always be grateful for...*

DATE / /

To this day, the *silliest thing* you've done has been...

DATE ___ / ___ / ___

The *best adventure* we've had together...

WHAT WE DID

WHY IT WAS THE BEST

DATE / /

If you *could read this,* here's what I'd say to you right now...

DATE / /

You don't know this, but you were *there for me...*

WHERE I WAS EMOTIONALLY

WHAT YOU DID

HOW IT HELPED ME

AFFIRMATION

You are the *calm* at the end of my *hardest days.*

DATE / /

A *little routine* we have that makes our days better...

DATE / /

Our *favourite games* we play together...

THE GAME	WHY WE LOVE IT

THE GAME	WHY WE LOVE IT

DATE / /

Looking back, I realise *we've both changed* by...

DATE / /

One of my *happiest memories* with you is...

DATE / /

If I could *describe your personality* in three simple words, they would be...

WORD ONE

WORD TWO

WORD THREE

DATE / /

Even when nothing's happening, *being near you* makes me feel...

BECAUSE

AFFIRMATION

You show me
a kind of love
that asks for
nothing
in return.

DATE / /

The way I know *you love me without question* is because you...

DATE / /

I love the way you *beg for something* because...

DATE / /

If you could *talk*, I think you would say...

DATE / /

You've *taught me* so much about...

DATE / /

Your *funniest* little habits are…

HABIT ONE

HABIT TWO

DATE / /

Your expressions always give away *how you feel*, especially when...

DATE / /

Your *favourite* toys

MOST CHEWED

STILL SQUEAKS *(somehow)*

TOTALLY DESTROYED, BUT YOU LOVED IT

FAVOURITE RIGHT NOW

Roselle

The guide dog who walked through fire...

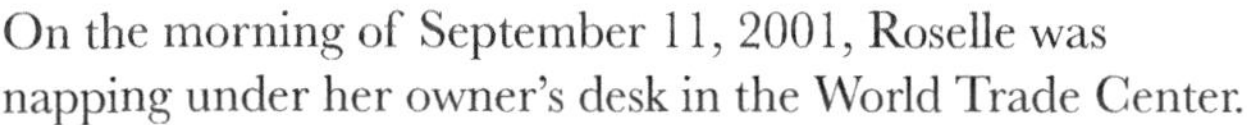

On the morning of September 11, 2001, Roselle was napping under her owner's desk in the World Trade Center.

When disaster struck, she stayed calm.

Despite smoke, chaos, and loud noises, she guided her blind owner down 78 flights of stairs…

step

by

step.

But she didn't stop there.

Roselle led him out of the building, across crowded streets, and even calmed others along the way. She helped guide 30 people to safety that day, never once faltering.

She couldn't see the destruction, but she knew exactly what to do: stay close, stay focused, and keep her person safe.

DATE / /

A *small thing* I want to thank you for today is…

DATE / /

You *changed my life* without even trying by...

DATE / /

Things I *never want to forget* about you…

DATE / /

The *best surprise* you've ever given me is...

DATE / /

That time *you looked at me* in a way that said everything...

WHAT WAS THE LOOK?

WHAT DID I THINK YOU WERE TRYING TO TELL ME?

HOW DID I FEEL?

DATE / /

I love when we *spend time together* doing...

DATE ____ / ____ / ____

Our *perfect day together* would look like...

MORNING

AFTERNOON

EVENING

AFFIRMATION

You are,
and always
will be,
*my greatest
companion.*

DATE / /

You always know how to make *an ordinary day feel special* when you...

DATE / /

When you're *simply lying beside me*, I feel...

BECAUSE...

DATE / /

My *favourite part* of our daily routine is...

DATE / /

A little thing you do that never fails to *make me smile*…

IT MAKES ME SMILE BECAUSE

DATE / /

Before you *and* after you

BEFORE YOU CAME INTO MY LIFE

AFTER YOU CAME INTO MY LIFE

DATE / /

Even *years from now*, I'll smile when I remember...

AFFIRMATION

You don't speak,
but you've
taught me more
than words ever
could.

DATE / /

5 things I've *learned from you*

ONE

TWO

THREE

FOUR

FIVE

DATE / /

Every day, I'm *thankful* that you...

DATE / /

That time you were *really guilty*...

WHAT HAPPENED

HOW I KNEW YOU WERE GUILTY

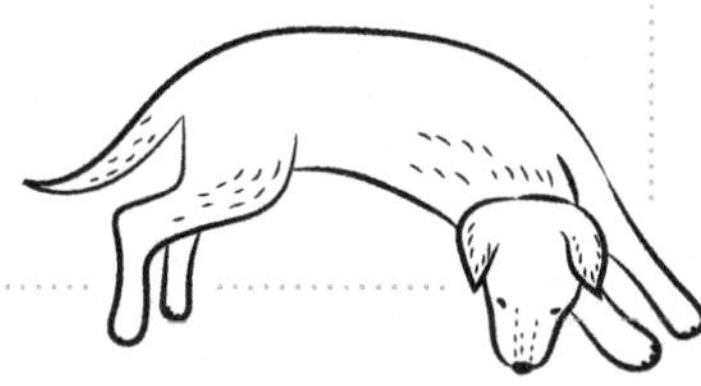

DATE / /

A moment when you made me *laugh until I cried...*

DATE / /

Let's revisit *one special moment* with you…

WHERE WERE WE?

WHAT HAPPENED?

WHY IT STAYS WITH ME

DATE / /

I never want to *take for granted* the way you...

DATE / /

One of the *quirkiest things* you do is…

Captain

The dog who never left his owner's side...

In a small town in Argentina, a German Shepherd named Capitan disappeared shortly after his owner passed away.

The family searched everywhere, until they found him lying beside the man's grave. Somehow, Capitan had found the cemetery on his own.

And once he was there, he never left.

For more than ten years, Capitan returned to the gravesite every evening. Rain or shine, he curled up next to his person.

No one taught him to do it.

He just knew.

His quiet loyalty became known across the country. But to him, it wasn't a grand gesture.

It was simply where he was meant to be.

DATE / /

That time you made *life feel lighter...*

WHAT FELT HEAVY?

HOW DID YOU MAKE IT LIGHTER?

DATE / /

One small thing you do that *makes me feel seen...*

DATE / /

The *way you greet me* still surprises me because...

DATE / /

Today, you've helped me *become more present* by...

DATE / /

When I *think about our bond*, the first word that comes to mind is…

WHY I CHOSE THIS WORD

DATE / /

I'm not sure how, but *being with you helped me...*

DATE / /

You don't need to try - you already *make everything better* just by doing these small things...

AFFIRMATION

You have a way of being *exactly what I need*, without even trying.

DATE / /

If I could *bottle up your energy* today, it would feel like...

DATE / /

When we're *outside together*, the world feels different with you by my side...

WHAT I SEE

WHAT I HEAR

WHAT I FEEL

DATE / /

Things I've *noticed more* about life because of you

YOU OPENED MY EYES TO

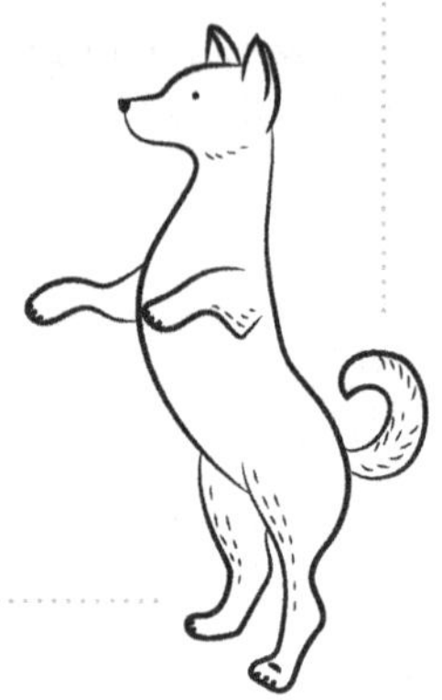

DATE / /

Your *cheeky* habit that I *secretly adore*...

THE HABIT

THE LAST TIME YOU DID IT

DATE / /

If I could *tell the world* one thing about you, it would be...

DATE / /

The little things you do that *make my heart melt* are…

LITTLE THING #1

LITTLE THING #2

LITTLE THING #3

LITTLE THING #4

AFFIRMATION

I'm a
better version
of myself
because I have
a dog *like you.*

DATE / /

Since you *came into my life*, I've become more...

DATE / /

The way *you look at me* in certain moments says...

DATE / /

You always *seem to know* when I need...

DATE / /

You have the *best reactions*...

WHENEVER I DO THIS

YOUR REACTION IS

DATE / /

A moment with you that always *makes me smile...*

DATE / /

If I could s*peak dog*, I would tell you…

DATE ___ / ___ / ___

My *favourite sounds* from you...

Smoky

The tiny war dog with a huge heart...

During World War II, soldiers in New Guinea discovered a Yorkshire Terrier in an abandoned foxhole. This tiny dog that was barely 2kg, became a legend.

Smoky kept soldiers company, performed tricks to boost morale, and even helped run communication lines by crawling through narrow pipes.

She dodged

bullets,

parachuted from

p
l
a
n
e
s

and never left her handler's side.

Her bravery wasn't loud, it was steady. Quiet courage, in a very small package.

DATE   /   /

Your top three *tricks*

FIRST TRICK

SECOND TRICK

THIRD TRICK

DATE / /

You don't ask for much, but *you give me so much* by...

DATE / /

You find *joy in the little things* such as...

BECAUSE OF YOU, I'M LEARNING TO...

DATE / /

You've shown me what *loyalty* really means by...

DATE / /

If I had to describe *our daily life together,* it would be like...

DATE / /

Quiet moments with you are *golden* because...

DATE / /

You've helped me become *more present*

BEFORE: I USED TO RUSH THROUGH...

NOW: I SLOW DOWN WHEN...

THANKS TO YOU, I'VE LEARNED TO NOTICE...

AFFIRMATION

You have taught me how to be more *present*, *patient* and *joyful*.

DATE / /

When I picture us together *years from now*, I imagine...

DATE / /

I felt *closest to you* when...

WHY IT MATTERED TO ME

DATE / /

You know *exactly how to get your way* when you...

...and I'll fall for it every time

DATE / /

A walk with you *isn't just a walk*, it's...

DATE / /

I feel *lucky to have you* in my life because...

DATE / /

One memory of you that always *brings me comfort*...

THE MEMORY

WHY IT BRINGS ME COMFORT

AFFIRMATION

You have *never needed words* to show me what *love* looks like.

DATE / /

All the different ways *you show your love* for me

DATE / /

Your weird habits *I can't explain* but love anyway...

HABIT ONE

HABIT TWO

HABIT THREE

DATE / /

Something *simple* you do every day that makes me smile...

DATE / /

You may *not be able to read this*, but I hope you know...

DATE / /

I never want to *forget* how you...

DATE / /

Today, I'm *grateful* that you...

DATE / /

The different ways you *greet me* when I come home...

Gobi

The stray dog who ran a marathon and found a home...

In the middle of China's Gobi Desert, a stray dog began to follow an ultra-marathon runner named Dion.

She trotted beside him day after day,

across scorching heat,

running rivers,

and rough terrain.

He hadn't planned to adopt a dog, but she made the decision easy. After the race, Dion arranged to bring her home to the UK.

They named her Gobi, after the desert where their story began.

Sometimes, the ones who are meant to find you…

…just do.

DATE / /

The top three things *I admire* about your personality

ONE

TWO

THREE

DATE / /

Today, you were *so cute* because...

DATE / /

What I love most about *waking up and seeing you* is…

DATE / /

If I could take you *anywhere in the world*, we would go to...

HOW WE WOULD SPEND THE DAY

DATE / /

All the things I'm *so proud of you* for…

DATE / /

I hope you *always know* that...

DATE / /

When I'm with you, I feel *most like myself*

WHO I AM WITH YOU

WHY THAT VERSION OF ME FEELS TRUE

AFFIRMATION

You *don't care* who I am to the world. You love me *just as I am*.

DATE / /

Our *little rituals* mean so much to me, like when we...

DATE / /

You've *challenged me* in ways I didn't expect.

THE MOMENT

WHAT YOU TAUGHT ME ABOUT MYSELF

HOW THIS DEEPENED OUR BOND

DATE ____ / ____ / ____

Our *favourite place* we always go together is...

THE PLACE

WHY IT'S OUR FAVOURITE

DATE / /

Today, I want to *thank you* for...

DATE / /

I *find comfort* in knowing that you will always...

DATE / /

I will always *appreciate your loyalty...*

THE MOMENT THAT PROVED IT

WHY I'LL NEVER FORGET IT

AFFIRMATION

When I look at you, all I see *is home*.

DATE / /

To me, you will *always be home...*

WHAT MAKES YOU FEEL LIKE HOME?

THE MOMENT WHEN I FELT THIS MOST DEEPLY

DATE ___ / ___ / ___

If I could *freeze a moment in time*, I would relive…

DATE / /

If you *could read this now*, I would tell you…

DATE / /

As you grow older, I want to *cherish every moment* because…

DATE / /

The *naughtiest thing* you did

WHAT YOU DID

MY REACTION

WHAT YOU DID TO MAKE UP FOR IT

DATE / /

If *soulmates exist* between humans and dogs, I know you're mine because…

DATE / /

Because of you, I have learned to *appreciate*…

Swansea Jack

The dog who saved lives from the water...

In the 1930s, a black retriever mix named Swansea Jack lived near the River Tawe in Wales.

One day, he saw a boy fall into the water and without hesitation, Jack leapt in and pulled him to shore.

That wasn't a one-time act.

Over the next few years, Swansea Jack saved more than 25 people from drowning. Locals would see him

pacing the banks,

always watching,

always ready.

He was awarded medals, praised in newspapers, and named "Dog of the Century."

But to his town, he was more than a hero.

He was family.

DATE / /

The *sweetest thing* you've done...

WHAT YOU DID

HOW I FELT

DATE / /

Sometimes, I just *look at you* and think…

DATE / /

The day you came home, *everything changed* because…

DATE / /

I wish you knew *how much it means to me* when you…

DATE / /

All the things you do when *you want attention*...

DATE / /

I think we *understand each other best* when…

DATE / /

Small moments I loved with you today...

AFFIRMATION

Every day
with you is
a small,
beautiful gift.

DATE / /

Thank you for always…

DATE / /

There is a peace I only feel *when you're near...*

THIS PEACE
FEELS LIKE

DATE / /

Today, you made me *chuckle* because...

WHAT YOU DID

WHY IT MADE ME CHUCKLE

DATE / /

You don't say a word, but *somehow I know*...

DATE / /

You may not speak my language, but I know *you understand me* when…

DATE / /

You bring *so much joy* into my life when you...

WHY IT BRINGS ME SO MUCH JOY

AFFIRMATION

My love
for you lives in
every corner
of our
time together.

DATE / /

What I'll *tuck into my heart* forever

A SOUND

A LOOK

A FEELING

DATE / /

All my *favourite things* about you...

DATE / /

The way you *comfort me* when I am having an off day is so special because…

DATE / /

You are the *funniest* when you…

DATE / /

How you act when you hear a *certain word*...

THE WORD

HOW YOU ACT

DATE / /

When I think back on *our time together,* what I want to remember most is…

DATE / /

What I *think you get up* to when I'm not at home...

DATE / /

When I picture us together *years from now*, I imagine...

AFFIRMATION

There will never be *enough words* for the *love I'll always carry* for you.

This might be the last page, but it's not the last thing I will ever say to you. *If you could read this*, this is what I want you to know...

DATE / /

DATE / /

Because love like
ours never really ends,
it just changes form.

Dear Dog Journals

www.deardogjournals.com

A catalogue record for this book is available from the National Library of Australia

ISBN 978-1-7641918-0-7

Made in the USA
Las Vegas, NV
30 July 2025